SHORT BLACKS are gems of recent
Australian writing – brisk reads that quicken
the pulse and stimulate the mind.

SHORT BLACKS

TRADITION, TRUTH & TOMORROW

GALARRWUY YUNUPINGU

SHORT BLACKS

Published by Black Inc.,
an imprint of Schwartz Publishing Pty Ltd
37–39 Langridge Street
Collingwood VIC 3066 Australia
enquiries@blackincbooks.com
www.blackincbooks.com

First published in the *Monthly*, December 2008.
This edition published 2015.

National Library of Australia Cataloguing-in-Publication entry:
Yunupingu, Galarrwuy, 1948– author.
Tradition, truth & tomorrow / Galarrwuy Yunupingu.
9781863957748 (paperback) 9781925203561 (ebook) Short blacks ; no.12.
Yunupingu, Galarrwuy, 1948–. Yolngu (Australian people).
305.89915

Cover and text design by Peter Long.

GALARRWUY YUNUPINGU is a
member of the Gumatj clan from
Yirrkala, in north-east Arnhem Land.
He played a key role in the battle for
indigenous land rights and has been
a strong advocate for Aboriginal
Australians. He was Australian of the
Year in 1978, and was made a Member of
the Order of Australia in 1985 for services
to the Aboriginal community.

I was born in 1948 at Gunyangara, a beach on a beautiful headland near what is now known as Nhulunbuy, in north-east Arnhem Land. My father was Mungurrawuy Yunupingu, of the Gumatj clan, and my mother, Makurrngu, was of the Galpu clan. My parents gave me the name Galarrwuy, which means 'the area on the horizon where the sea merges with the sky'. As I grew older my father would call me Djingarra, which means 'crystal clear'. My elder sisters still call me this special name.

My father's father was Nikunu. His totem was a sacred rock, an unbreakable rock – *Yunupingu* – a name that my grandfather gave to his son, Mungurrawuy, who passed it to all his children. My totem is fire, rock and the saltwater crocodile. The crocodile – *baru* – is a flame of fire: the mouth, the teeth and the jaw are the fire and its jaw is death. It is always burning, and through it I have energy, power – strength.

My land is that of the Gumatj clan nation, which is carefully defined, with boundaries and borders set out in the maps of our minds and, today, on *djurra*, or paper. We have our own laws, repeated in ceremonial song cycles and known to all members of our clan nation. Sung into our ears as babies, disciplined into our bodies through dance and movement – we have learnt and inherited the knowledge of our fathers and mothers. We live on our land, with our laws, speaking our language, sharing our beliefs and living our lives bound together with the other great clan nations of the Gove Peninsula: Rirratjingu, Djapu, Wangurri, Dhalwangu, Mangalili, Madarrpa, Marra-kulu, Dartiwuy, Ngaymil, Gumatj, Galpu, Djambarrpuyngu, Dhudi-Djapu.

These are the 13 clans of the Gove Peninsula, in east Arnhem Land. Each is independent and proud; each is bound to the others through the moieties of Yirritja and Dhuwa. I am Yirritja and my clan is balanced by the Dhuwa clans, my mother

groups, most importantly the Galpu, Rirratjingu and Marrakulu clans.

The clans of east Arnhem Land join
me in acknowledging no king, no queen,
no church and no state. Our allegiance is to
each other, to our land and to the ceremonies
that define us. It is through the ceremonies
that our lives are created. These ceremonies record and pass on the laws that give us
ownership of the land and of the seas, and
the rules by which we live. Our ceremonial
grounds are our universities, where we gain
the knowledge that we need. The universities
work to a moon cycle, with many different
levels of learning and different 'inside' ceremonies for men and women: from the new
moon to the full moon, we travel the song
cycles that guide the life and the essence

of the clan – keeping all in balance, giving our people their meaning. It is the only cycle of events that can ever give a Yolngu person – someone from north-east Arnhem Land – the full energy that he or she requires for life. Without this learning, Yolngu can achieve nothing; they are nobody.

As a clan we seek that moment in the ceremonial cycle where all is equal and in balance. Where older men have guided the younger ones and, in turn, taken knowledge from their elders; where no one is better than anyone else, everyone is equal, performing their role and taking their duties and responsibilities – then the ceremony is balanced and the clan moves in unison: there is no female, no male, no little ones and no big ones; we are all the same.

My inner life is that of the Yolngu song cycles, the ceremonies, the knowledge, the law and the land. This is *yothu yindi*. Balance. Wholeness. Completeness. A world designed in perfection, founded on the beautiful simplicity of a mother and her newborn child; as vibrant and as dynamic as the estuary where the saltwaters meet the freshwaters, able to give you everything you need.

I step back to the 1950s. I am a small boy, maybe eight years old, able to tell the difference between right and wrong. An event is to take place at Yirrkala and members of the 13 clans are called together. Every man, woman and child is given clean clothes and dresses for the occasion, and they come together with pretty flowers in their hands, dressed up cleanly. All are told to stand in a line, from the bottom of the hill to the top of the hill, to greet the chairman of the board of the Australian Synod of the Methodist Church. And he arrives in a four-wheel-drive with other people who jump out of their cars and are received by the local people. I remember this occasion perfectly well. We just stood there for show, dressed prettily, holding pretty flowers, to give a so-called welcome to the Methodist Church. The vehicles came to rest, the dignitaries got out, they received their flowers, they smiled, then they left and that was that. The clan leaders stood there expecting something that would acknowledge them and respect them, an exchange or a gift in return – but they received nothing. We were badly caught up that day and a poor example was set.

Now it is the early 1960s and a man called Harry Giese, the so-called protector of

Aborigines in the Northern Territory, stands on a 44-gallon drum at the Yirrkala airport. He has called some people together to give them news – I am one of those people; my father is there also; Roy and Mawalan Marika; the Djapu leaders, too. A mine will be built here at Yirrkala, he tells us. It will mine the dirt that we stand on – our soil. The mining companies are coming and they will mine the land. They will take all the land and the boundary of that land will run to the edge of Yirrkala, and Yirrkala will be badly affected. Giese talks for 20 minutes, then he gets in his car and drives away. This is the first mining agreement on the Gove Peninsula.

My father sent me to school, although he worried that I might lose my Gumatj identity. I had a good teacher, Mr Ron

Crocksford, who kept pestering Mum and Dad to keep me at school and who worked overtime on my learning. As I received my education from my clan leaders and from the *balanda* teachers, I watched as the world changed. Inevitably the miners came and started their work.

As I grew up I was recognised and set apart by my father. He set out tasks for me and challenged me in everything. I went to Bible college in Brisbane for two years but I returned always to the ceremonies and the law – in the end, I turned my back on the church and their god. I dedicated myself, under the direction of my father and the older men, to a Yolngu future.

It is 1977. My father is still alive and I am on a boat with a new prime minister, Malcolm

Fraser. He has defeated Gough Whitlam, who first met my family when he was a pilot in World War II. With me is Toby Gangale, the senior Gundjehmi leader, steering us to a place where barramundi swim. Fraser has asked us to fish with him, and we hope there are words we can say to him that will halt his changes to the land-rights laws and overturn the government's decision to mine at Ranger. But Fraser only thinks about the fish. The fish bite and Fraser starts to pull them in. "Look at this one!" he yells. I bait his line again. Toby is silent. "And again – a bigger one." He baits his own line now – getting the hang of it. "You beauty, a barramundi!" All the time I try and put words in his mind about the importance of land, about the importance of respect, about giving things back in a proper way, not a halfway thing. But he has his mind on other things – he's not listening; he doesn't have to. He just keeps catching barramundi, enjoying himself.

On his deathbed, as his spirit started its journey to Badu, the spirit land, my father handed me his clapsticks and his authority. My senior family members saw the passing and told of it throughout the clan nations – it was the news of the day in the Yolngu world. It was 1979 and I was 31 years old. The year before I had been awarded an honour by the Australian nation: I was their Australian of the Year. I was the chairman of a new land council, the Northern Land Council, soon to be the most powerful in the nation. I had negotiated with prime ministers and men of state. I was a singer and a songwriter, a dancer and a painter. I had my father's clapsticks and with them I was sure that I could master the future.

I am with another new prime minister, Bob Hawke, at Barunga. Many clans, connected by distant but powerful songlines, have performed ceremony for this prime minister. It's 1988 and I've known Bob Hawke for many years. He had come to the Northern Territory to visit me when he was the president of the ACTU and, over a beer in Anula, I had told him that he had the common touch and that one day he would be the prime minister. At Barunga he is emotional and I am emotional as we embrace on the ceremonial ground. This is how it should be, I think. And I hear his words that there will be a treaty. A treaty! My heart leaps.

A few years later I travel to Canberra to hang a painting that was dreamed on that day:

the Barunga Statement. I think that I am in Canberra for a celebration but it is a funeral – it is Bob's last day as prime minister and he sheds a tear as he hangs the painting. I am sure that his tears are for his own failure – we have no treaty; his promise was hollow and he has not delivered – but they are genuine tears from a genuine man who tried leadership and was caught out by politics.

It is 1994. Mabo has been and gone and is now a soft, useless law. At Eva Valley in 1993 I sat with many clan leaders from the North, and we talked about Mabo and set out our position. No one listened; there was too much talk going on in Canberra; I didn't see any landowners there negotiating, only big talkers. Then I see on television the politicians in parliament crying and kissing each other. What is this? I think to myself.

*I wonder about Paul Keating, a prime min-
ister I never really met – if anyone could have
done something, surely Keating could've, I think.*

*We're celebrating the twentieth anniversary
of the Land Rights Act at the Old Parliament
House. There is a new prime minister, John
Howard, who has just been elected and he is
looking to deliver something to the new Australian people. I am sitting at breakfast and I hear
a radio tell me that the prime minister has taken
millions of dollars of funding for housing and
community programs. He is sending auditors
and investigators to check us all out.*

*Later I sit at a long table, talking about
'reconciliation'. Treaty has become reconciliation. There is all this talk about nothing. It is
not connected to the real goings-on. Eventually
I can't stand it any longer. I get up and leave the*

talkers to their talking and go back to Arnhem Land. Later, I send in my letter of resignation.

I am seeing now that too much of the past is for nothing. I have walked the corridors of power; I have negotiated and cajoled and praised and begged prime ministers and ministers, travelled the world and been feted; I have opened the doors to men of power and prestige; I have had a place at the table of the best and the brightest in the Australian nation – and at times success has seemed so close, yet it always slips away. And behind me, in the world of my father, the Yolngu world is always under threat, being swallowed up by whitefellas.

This is a weight that is bearing down on me; it is a pressure that I feel now every moment of my life – it frustrates me and drives me crazy; at night it is like a splinter in my mind. The solutions to the future, simple though I thought they were, have become harder and harder to grasp. I have learnt from experience that nothing is ever what it seems.

It is 2007. I am at the Garma Festival, surrounded by Aboriginal leaders from around Australia. They have come to meet me at my request – a challenge has been laid down by the commonwealth government, called an intervention.

John Howard is leading a government that is taking this hard action. I have been told that my land rights will be taken away and for me that is the end – for weeks now I feel a sickness creeping into my body; I have hardly slept in the past week. The Labor Party is with Howard.

I meet Jenny Macklin. It is clear to me that she has her instructions. I think about the old people in their clean clothes holding flowers and, under a bower shelter, I am hard on Jenny with words like fire, but she does not budge. I throw my all at her; my sisters speak to her in language, I interpret, as does my favourite niece, the late Ms Marika, but she will not budge – she cannot.

That night I carve message sticks with my daughter, asking for a meeting with John Howard and Kevin Rudd at Garma. I reason that this must be the next step – to bring them to Aboriginal land for the clan nations to address them. Not with flowers, but with spears if need be. The other leaders fight over who will carry the sticks: I want my friend Jack Thompson to take the sticks, but others want to take on this task. I make a mistake – I empower others to *speak for me. A delegation goes to Canberra but they do not meet with Howard or his minister, Mal Brough. Rudd agrees to meet with us, but he is steered away from Garma and the clan nations. Later, I hear that Jenny had booked her ticket to Garma to meet again with us but the meeting was foiled.*

The ALP caucus convenes and they vote to support Howard, with a bit of lip-service for good measure. I wait until late into the night, still camped at Garma. When I receive the news about the caucus decision, I ask to see Noel Pearson.

I'm back at Gulkula, the Garma site. Noel Pearson has come and he tells me about his vision. He seeks a balance in the balanda *world in its treatment of Aboriginal people. A synthesis, he calls it, between Left and Right. Only when*

*we have this balance can we go upwards, he
tells me. He speaks my language but I am not
yet convinced. Messages come to me from other
leaders from outside east Arnhem Land and they
say: Wait – Kevin Rudd will win the election.
But this time I decide I won't play that game
and be captured by one side of politics; I will
stand in the middle if I can. I ask Noel to contact
Mal Brough. I realise that my land rights have
not been taken away, and I wonder about those
who refused to meet with Brough and kept Rudd
away from me. I want in on this discussion: I
want to meet this man who has made such a
noise and who says such incredible things, to see
what he is really made of.*

Mal Brough came and he drove out to
meet me. I waited for him at the place of
my fathers, Dhanaya. I waited for Mal on

my father's land, looking over my mother's clan's waters – surrounded by memory and feeling. This is a place where freshwater, stirred up by the sacred stingray, meets saltwater. It is a rich, vibrant place, full of life. And for a fleeting moment, on this land, overlooking Port Bradshaw, with my family around me, we talked as men should – about the future of children and of failures and frustrations, and how we could turn it all around with action. He was frustrated and I was frustrated, and as fathers and leaders we saw a way forward. He talked straight and I talked straight, and each of us would honour our end of the discussion. We negotiated a lease that left me in charge of my land at my birthplace of Gunyangara – more in charge than I had ever been – while giving Canberra everything it wanted in terms of security and certainty. I supported his bans on drugs and kava, and promised him my support for the harsher parts of his plan if he could balance these measures with proper action. And I asked for one more thing: I wanted constitutional recognition, to bring my people in from the cold, bring us into the nation. There was a promise that he would talk with his prime minister.

*

Today, almost 30 years after my father passed away, I still hold his clapsticks and I am the leader of my clan – with other senior family members I am the keeper and teacher of our song cycles, our ceremonies, our laws and our future. I care for and protect my clan. But I have not mastered the future. I find that I now spend my days worrying about how I can protect the present from the future. I feel the future moving in on the Yolngu world, the Gumatj world, like an inevitable tide, except every year the tide rises further, moving up on us, threatening to drown us under the water, unable to rise again. The water sands under our feet shift and move so often – the land to which we can reach out is often distant, unknown.

I look around me at the Yolngu world. I worry about the lives of the little ones that I see around me, including my own children – my youngest daughter is barely eight years old. I have more than a dozen grandchildren. I look back now on a lifetime of effort and I see that we have not moved very far at all. For all the talk, all the policy, all the events, all the media spectaculars and fine speeches, the gala dinners, what has been achieved? I have maintained the traditions, kept the law, performed my role – yet the Yolngu world is in crisis; we have stood still. I look around me and I feel the powerlessness of all our leaders. All around me are do-gooders and no-hopers – can I say this? *Whitefellas. Balanda.* They all seem to be one and the same sometimes: talking, talking, talking – smothering us – but with no vision to guide them; holding all the power, all the money, all the knowledge for what to do and how to work the white world. Only on the ceremonial ground do our leaders still lead – everywhere else we are simply paid lip-service. Or bound up in red tape.

And the 'gap' that politicians now talk of grows larger as we speak, as I talk: as the next session of parliament starts or as the next speech is given by the next politician, the gap gets wider. I don't think anyone except the few of us who have lived our lives in the Aboriginal world understand this task that is called 'closing the gap'.

There is no one in power who has the experience to know these things. There is not one federal politician who has any idea about the enormity of the task. And how could they? Who in the senior levels of the commonwealth public service has lived through these things? Who in the parliament? No one speaks an Aboriginal language, let alone has the ability to sit with a young man or woman and share that person's experience and find out what is really in their heart. They have not raised these children in their arms, given them everything they have, cared for them, loved them, nurtured them. They have not had their land stolen, or their rights infringed, or their laws broken. They do not bury the dead as we bury our dead.

*

I am a Gumatj man; I am fire; and that fire must burn until there is nothing left. That is what I have left to give to my family.

The future is my responsibility. I have brought my family back around me, taking what we can from where we can, working with people who will help us practically and in an honest way.

I have started to rebuild Garrathiya, our cattle station near Dhanaya, which sat still for many years. New yards are being built, fences are being fixed, weeds are being sprayed and a dormitory has been constructed out of local timber. Fifteen of the clan's young men are at Garrathiya or Dhanaya.

We are now harvesting our trees, carefully picking the trees; we have set up a mill and are cutting our own timber. With this timber, grown from our land, we are starting to build our own houses. No one in government has come to my aid, but that is OK – that is the way it should be. We will keep building these houses with our own timber, our own labour and with help from those who wish to help us. My family tells me that now they will build a market garden to grow food at Garrathiya, and my nieces have started their art again, asking me to help them buy materials for their efforts. My big sister, Gulumbu, has a healing centre and is teaching young girls while treating *balanda* women.

I am finally in formal negotiations with the mining company Rio Tinto, which inherited Harry Giese's mining agreement and whose predecessors took so much from our land – billions of dollars – leaving us very little. I have worked with their senior people and committed to a new deal that will, hopefully, bring greater economic opportunity for north-east Arnhem Land.

I have purchased a fishing boat with our royalty money and hope this will be a pathway to a fishing industry. I am leasing my land and putting that money towards these enterprises. I plan a property development, a marina, a new town built by Yolngu on Yolngu land.

This is about building our own lives, our own communities. If I can't give that opportunity to my clan, no one else can. What they achieve will be for them, out of their hard work, for their happiness and security – not for some outsider.

It's July 2008 and I wait for the new prime minister, Kevin Rudd. An event is taking place at Yirrkala and I have called the leaders of the 13 clans together. No children or young people will participate, only leaders, men and women who have proved themselves: dilak. *By my side are Djiniyini Gondarra and the leaders of the Elcho clans, Richard Gandhuwuy and Danga- tanga Gondarra, Butharripi Gurruwiwi. Wilson Ganambarr, Gali Gurruwiwi, Djekurr Guyula and Timmy Burrawanga are there. Laklak and Dhuwarrwarr Marika are there, too, along with the great old man from Gan Gan, Garrawin Gumana. My cousin Banambi Wunungmurra brings the prime minister down to us. We have a petition for him.*

Nhanaburru, wangkanmala bapurru dhimirrunguru, arnhemland, nganaburrungu ngurrngu dilak mala, nganthun yukurra nhuna 26th Prime Minister Australia-wu. Nhukala ganydjarr'yu nhunhi nhe ngurrungu walalangu malangura nhuma walala rrambangi, Australian Parliament-ngura, ga ngurrungu Dharuk-mirri nhangu Garraywu Queen Elizabeth-gu, yurru nhandarryun-marama djinawa-lili Australian-dhu luku-wu rom-dhu yurru dharangan ga galmuma nganapurrungu dhangang ga bukmak nha-mala nhanapurrungu:

– Nhanapurrungu walnga-mirri dhukarry ngudhudal-yana.

– Nhanapurrungu, wanga, wanga-ngaraka ga nguy gapu, ngunhi dhimirrunguru, arnhemland.

– *Dharrima gungnharra, warkthunara, luku-nydja rrupiya-yu wanga-wuy-ga gapu-wuy ga dhangangnha-yana ga lukunydjana yana.*
– *Dharray walnga-wuy ga djaka yurru nhanapurrung-gala-nguwu djamarrkuli-wu yalalangu-wu.*

Dhuwalanydja rom dhuwalana bilina.

Dhuwalanydja rom wawungu wanga-wuy ngandarryunmarama Australian-gala bapurrulili.

Nganapurru marrliliyama nhukula ngurru-warryun-narayngu, marr yurru Commonwealth Parliament ngurru warrwun ga dharangan dhuwala rom ga marryuwak gumana dhayutakumana lukunydja rom.

We, the united clans of East Arnhem land, through our most senior *dilak*, do humbly petition you, the 26th Prime Minister of Australia, in your capacity as the first amongst equals in the Australian Parliament, and as the chief adviser to Her Majesty Queen Elizabeth the Second, to secure within the Australian Constitution the recognition and protection of our full and complete right to:

– Our way of life in all its diversity;
– Our property, being the lands and waters of East Arnhem land;
– Economic independence, through the proper use of the riches of our land and waters in all their abundance and wealth;

– Control of our lives and responsibility for
   our children's future.

These rights are self-evident.

These rights are fundamental to our place
within the Australian nation.

We ask for your leadership to have the Commonwealth Parliament start the process of
recognition of these rights through serious
constitutional reform.

The ceremonial ground is prepared by the Dhuwa clan nations, ready for the Yirritja. The Gumatj clan nation performs for the prime minister a special ceremony: *gurtha* – fire. The men move in unison – all perfect, all equal, all united. There is thunder overhead, and rain, and we become one. My brother Mandawuy's wife, Yalmay, of the Rirratjingu clan nation, reads the petition to the assembly in language. Her voice is strong and beautiful. The children of Yirrkala gather and take the petition to the prime minister and he welcomes it, holds it, and admires the design. He shakes my hand. The ceremony finishes and I leave Yirrkala.

*

Knowing these things might help readers to understand that the Northern Territory emergency intervention – any government intervention or program, while well intentioned and even when backed by money – will not fully solve anything. The intervention has simply started a process that, if the history I know is any guide, will end up failing. Not because of the reasons given by those well-meaning people in the cities, or those that have made a life out of being in the Aboriginal industry, or those who study, analyse and explore our lives. The intervention is good for these people – black and white – because it gives them oxygen, so they can show their importance and expertise. You must not listen to these people; they have let their ignorance get in the way of their thinking. The truth is, the intervention is about the welfare economy and the relationship between governments and Aboriginal people, and any good is fading as the old ways of doing business are reasserting their dominance. Soon even the talk will stop – there will be no more interest – and it will just be red tape again, business as usual.

I have a letter from Jenny Macklin about the lease that I negotiated with Mal Brough and Dr Peter Shergold, but there is no urgency there anymore. When I read it, I felt like dropping it to the floor. I want certainty and a solid foundation but I sense that the public servants, so-called, do not like my lease, never did. They want me to talk to *them* – to give them their power back.

They hated that I talked with a minister or a prime minister, or that the new minister thinks I might have some important things to say. These red-tape men don't like my lease, because it leaves the power with Yolngu and they only know power from Canberra, or Darwin. They have us tied up in red tape at every level, and the minister too, I think.

Today, nearly all my people live in shambling, broken-down places with poor houses, poor roads, bad schools, little or no health care, with whitefellas in a welfare industry who service us when they can, if they want. We are captives of welfare, which means we are wards of the state relying on handouts from public servants to get by, and therefore our lives are controlled by governments and public servants who can do what they want, when they feel like it. And people suffer from their neglect – just look at our communities and the lives too many of our people are forced to endure. Although the wealth of the Australian nation has been taken from our soil, our communities and homelands bear no resemblance to the great towns and metropolises of the modern Australian nation. The intervention and what it promises is important. I do not set it aside completely. But I tell my family now: no government, no politician, no journalist or TV man, no priest, no greenie, no well-meaning dreamer from the city is going to put your life right for you. I have committed my clan to the future and my family supports me, even as it struggles with everyday life. And I will continue this commitment.

I will continue my work on my land, building a future. It is the only thing that is certain to me now and I want to advance while I can. I am trying to light the fire in our young men and women. We are setting fires to our own lives as we really should, and the flame will burn and intensify – an immense smoke, cloud-like and black, will arise, which will send off a signal and remind people that we, the Gumatj people, are the people of the fire. This will draw the other clan nations, all of which are related to the fire: the Blue Mud Bay people, all the way through to the people as far off as Maningrida. There are people of the fire around Alice Springs – and I reach out to them, too. We can then burn united, together.

*

This has been a hard story to tell, as it is a story of disappointment and frustration.

I still hope that there will be a happy ending to this story. But the big happy ending is out of my hands now. All I can do is this: in a few months I want to invite the prime minister to come to Arnhem Land and sit with the *dilak*. We will start small, and I hope he brings his family with him. If the prime minister agrees, the Opposition leader might join us. There is a small beach near a beautiful headland where we could start this process, light a small fire. We would then move out onto the peninsula, stopping at the important sites and places. We will need a few days, maybe a week, and the *dilak* can talk slowly and carefully and we can each commit to the future.

I will then travel to Canberra again, on only one condition. It will be at the invitation of the prime minister, Labor or Liberal – to me and the *dilak* of east Arnhem Land, and to the other Aboriginal leaders of the lands and waters of Australia. The invitation will be to join with him to hang the 2008 Yirrkala Petition on the wall of Parliament House, side by side with the 1988 Barunga Statement and the 1963 Bark Petition. And the prime minister will have in his hand a bill for introduction into the parliament. That bill will take all the wisdom and wishes of the three paintings and turn them into law, requiring a convention on all these matters, with a new constitution to be drafted and a New Settlement to be proposed to the Australian people. I am 60 years old and it is to this future, as set out in this essay, that I would pledge my final years.

THE WAR OF THE WORLDS
NOEL PEARSON

Noel Pearson considers the most confronting issue of Australian history: the question of genocide, in early Tasmania and elsewhere.

REGIONS OF THICK-RIBBED ICE
HELEN GARNER

Helen Garner tells the tale of a journey to Antarctica aboard the *Professor Molchanov*, spanning icebergs, tourism, time, photography and the many forms of desolation.

WWW.SHORTBLACKS.COM

THE BRAVE ONES
EAST TIMOR, 1999
JOHN BIRMINGHAM

John Birmingham's unflinching account of the Indonesian Army's Battalion 745 as it withdrew from East Timor after the 1999 independence vote, leaving a trail of devastation in its wake.

BOOZE TERRITORY
ANNA KRIEN

Anna Krien takes a clear-eyed look at Indigenous binge-drinking, and never fails to see the human dimension of an intractable problem, shining a light on its deep causes.

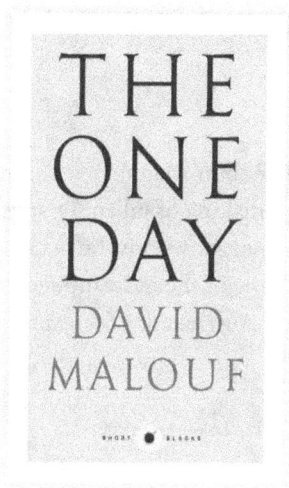

THE ONE DAY
DAVID MALOUF

SHORT ● BLACKS

David Malouf traces the meaning of Anzac Day and shows how what was once history has now passed into legend, and how we have found in Anzac Day 'a truly national occasion.'

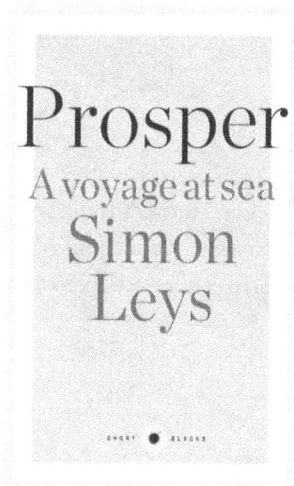

Prosper
A voyage at sea
Simon Leys

SHORT ● BLACKS

Simon Leys' exceptionally beautiful and elegiac essay about a summer spent on the crew of a tuna-fishing boat in Brittany.

CYPHERPUNK
REVOLUTIONARY
ON
JULIAN
ASSANGE
ROBERT
MANNE

SHORT ● BLACKS

Robert Manne reveals the
making of Julian Assange
and shows how he became
one of the most influential
Australians of our time.

KILLING THE
BLACK DOG
LES MURRAY

SHORT ● BLACKS

Les Murray's frank and
courageous account of his
struggle with depression.

NO FIXED ADDRESS
ROBYN DAVIDSON

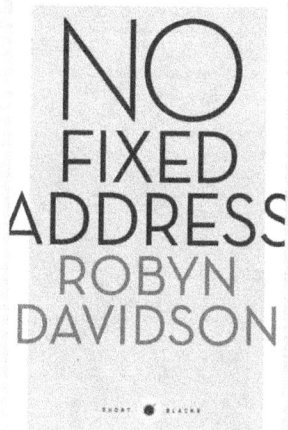

Robyn Davidson's fascinating and moving essay about nomads explores why, in times of environmental peril, the nomadic way with nature still offers valuable lessons.

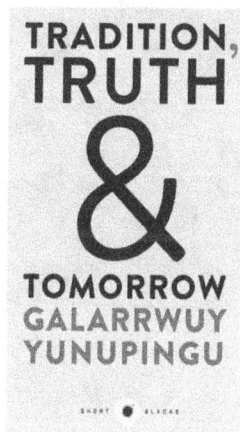

TRADITION, TRUTH & TOMORROW
GALARRWUY YUNUPINGU

Galarrwuy Yunupingu tells of his early life, his dealings with prime minsters, and how he learnt that nothing is ever what it seems.

WWW.SHORTBLACKS.COM

www.ingramcontent.com/pod-product-compliance
Lightning Source LLC
Chambersburg PA
CBHW052107270326
41931CB00012B/2923